ANGRY BIRDS™ STAR WARS®
ULTIMATE STICKER COLLECTION

HOW TO USE THIS BOOK

READ THE CAPTIONS, THEN FIND
THE STICKER THAT BEST FITS THE SPACE.
(HINT: CHECK THE STICKER LABELS FOR CLUES!)

•

DON'T FORGET THAT YOUR STICKERS CAN
BE STUCK DOWN AND PEELED OFF AGAIN.

•

THERE ARE LOTS OF FANTASTIC EXTRA STICKERS FOR
CREATING YOUR OWN SCENES THROUGHOUT THE BOOK.

LONDON, NEW YORK,
MELBOURNE, MUNICH, AND DELHI

Written by Simon Beecroft
Edited by Laura Gilbert
Editorial Assistance: Allison Singer
Designed by Lynne Moulding

First published in the United States in 2013 by
DK Publishing
375 Hudson Street, New York, New York 10014

10 9 8 7 6 5 4 3 2 1
001–187764–Mar/13

Page design copyright © 2013 Dorling Kindersley Limited

ISBN: 978-1-4654-0075-8

Color Reproduction by Altaimage in the UK
Printed and bound in China by L-Rex

Discover more at
www.dk.com

I'M C-3PYOLK THE DROID, AND I WELCOME YOU TO OUR WORLD IN PEACE.

I'M LARD VADER, AND I DON'T!

BATTLE FOR THE EGG

Somewhere in space there is a lot of anger. A group of angry Rebel Birds, including the strong Jedi, are in battle with the Pig Empire. The Empire's evil leader, Lard Vader, believes that the birds are hiding something strange and powerful. This mysterious thing holds the power to rule the world—The Egg.

RED SKYWALKER

Hardheaded and a bit clumsy, Red Skywalker is on a mission to find the Egg. But he can't do it alone—this bird needs help!

YODA BIRD

As wise as an owl, Jedi Yoda Bird is the only one who knows the mysterious secret of The Egg's true whereabouts.

LARD VADER

This greedy pig wants to find and eat The Egg and become the ruler of the entire universe! Will the birds get there first?

PIGTROOPERS

Mean and greedy, the Pigtroopers work for Emperor Piglatine. They make sure the greedy King Pig is well fed!

PIG STAR

The menacing Pig Star is a battle station built for one purpose: to stop the angry birds from locating The Egg first.

ANGRY BIRDS,
PLACE YOUR STICKERS
HERE AT YOUR PERIL!
THIS BATTLE STATION IS
ON LUNCH BREAK!

TATOOINE

The birds spend most of their time traveling through the galaxy, so it is good to come home—even if home is a harsh desert planet called Tatooine. Only the angriest, most bad-tempered birds spend time on its dusty desert surface, and they're getting angrier by the minute. Watch out—feathers may fly!

LOCAL BIRD
Red Skywalker lives a very dull and dreary life on Tatooine, until he joins the flock of Rebel Birds and gets in on the action!

OBI-WAN KABOOMI
Birds on Tatooine don't know that Obi-Wan is really a Jedi Knight in hiding. Now he is ready to spread his wings and join the Rebel Birds.

R2-EGG2

The fat-bellied astromech droid bird R2-EGG2 is oval for a reason—The Egg is hidden inside this friendly droid.

GOLDEN DROID

C-3PYOLK is a protocol droid and interpreter. He might bicker with R2-EGG2, but he is actually a Droid of Peace.

Pig Empire

A bunch of greedy, hungry pigs rule the Empire. They poke their snouts into everything in their desperate attempts to find The Egg before the Rebel Birds find it first. Not all the pigs know it but The Egg actually contains the Force, a special power with which to rule the galaxy.

Emperor Piglatine

Emperor Piglatine has banned candy and junk food throughout the whole universe. This King Pig wants to have it all for himself!

When I find The Egg, I'll eat it quicker than you can say, "Galactic Domination!"

Imperial recruit

Lard Vader was once a good Jedi warrior, but now he fights for the pigs. His Pigtroopers help him sniff out any danger.

TROOPERS

The Pig Empire's soldiers keep looking for junk food around the universe in order to deliver it to their ruler, Emperor Piglatine.

SIGN OF THE EMPIRE

Watch out—there's a snout about! Wherever the symbol of the Pig Empire appears, you can be sure that greedy pigs are nearby.

RED GUARDS

The feared red guards stand watch over the Pig Emperor. That spiked fork could cut through an egg with ease.

RED LIGHTSABER

Lightsabers are powered by crystals. The pigs' lightsabers have red blades and the birds' lightsabers have blue blades.

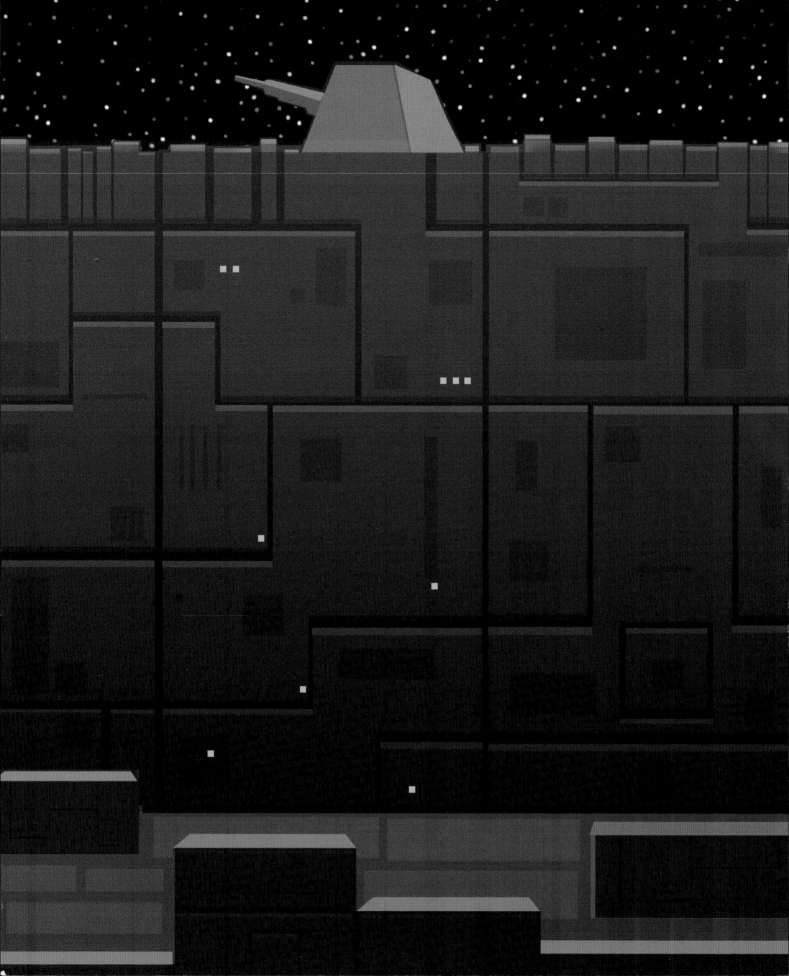

PIG STAR

The pigs have just got to find that Egg! To do so, they have built a giant battle station called the Pig Star. The well-armed Pig Star floats in space and looks thoroughly menacing. All around it fly the Pig Empire's spaceships. The Rebel Birds know they must destroy it at any cost!

FACE OF FEAR
The Pig Star is not only the largest pig-made battle station—it also looks like a pig with its huge snout and piggy ears! Scary!

VADER
Lard Vader wears a mysterious dark mask—no pig or angry bird has ever seen the face that hides underneath it.

PIG RIVALS
The Emperor and Vader rule side by side. But the Emperor doesn't know that Vader wants to rise above him in the pecking order.

TIE FIGHTER

The Pig Empire's main attack ship is the TIE fighter. TIE fighters swarm around like mosquitoes, but they are piggy to the core.

Once I find The Egg there will be only one choice: fried or omelette?

SECRET CHAMBER

Lard Vader likes to sit alone in his secret chamber and dream of finally locating and eating The Egg. Grunt, grunt!

VADER'S VEHICLE

Lard Vader's own TIE fighter is armed with green lightsabers. It is just a little bit faster and a little bit piggier than anyone else's.

Pig Army

The soldiers and pilots of the Pig Empire don't think for themselves. They merely follow orders and often fail in whatever they are trying to do. Sometimes they enlist the help of specialist bounty hunters like Boba Fatt, who can really manage to ruffle the birds' feathers.

WHEN MY HUNT IS OVER, I'M HAPPY TO BE PAID IN EGGS!

BOBA FATT
This mysterious character is a bounty hunter called Boba Fatt. He is specially trained to hunt and find birds for a fee.

FATT BACKPACK
Boba Fatt's jet-powered backpack gives him a lift when the battle is wearing him down. Maybe pigs *might* fly!

SCAREDY PIG

Pigtroopers are usually to be found in the middle of any battles and laser gunfights. However, even they are scared at times.

PIG PILOT

Pig Pilots fly TIE fighters and have special breathing masks to help them survive in space. They also wear the pig symbol with pride.

PIG COMMANDER

Pig Commanders give out orders to the rest of the Pigtroopers. They expect the troops to follow them like sheep.

THE BIRD REPUBLIC

A rebellious group of angry birds, including Red Skywalker, don't understand why they are being treated like outlaws. They might have bad tempers, but they don't have The Egg! Neither the birds nor the pigs know that The Egg is very near—it is inside the birds' servant robot R2-EGG2!

ROOKIE REBEL BIRD

Red Skywalker is committed to the rebellion. He believes he knows the secrets of the Egg. He just needs to find it to make sure . . .

PRINCESS ORGANA

Princess Stella Organa is one of the leaders of the Bird Republic. She expects everybody to obey her and is a bit of a drama queen.

SOMEONE HAS TO KEEP THIS FLOCK OF BIRDS IN CHECK!

JEDI WARRIOR

Obi-Wan Kaboomi is a Jedi warrior and uses his powers for good. He wants to protect The Egg even though he has no idea where it is.

CHUCK SOLO

Chuck "Ham" Solo got his nickname from smuggling junk food across the galaxy. He is a reckless gambler who is always in debt.

FEATHERY REBEL BIRD

The big bird with the flyaway feathers and ammunition belt is Terebacca. He is Ham Solo's trusted co-pilot and mechanic.

PIRATE AND PRINCESS

Why would a smuggler join the Rebellion? Ham Solo has taken a shine to the princess. Stella won't admit it but she likes him, too.

SMUGGLING TEAM

Famous junk food smuggler Chuck "Ham" Solo and his giant co-pilot Terebacca are a team. They fly together in their spaceship, they smuggle together, and they both join the Rebel Birds at the same time. It seems that birds of a feather really do flock together.

CLOSE BUDDIES
Ham Solo is the only one who truly understands what Terebacca is saying when he grunts and growls, even if it is just something silly.

GRRR NN GRAAAR GAR NNNNARRGH. GRNNN AAR GRNGRAAAA!

HAM'S SHIP
Ham Solo won his spaceship called the *Falcon* in a food fight with a rival smuggler. It can speed across the galaxy.

CONFIDENT BIRD

Ham brims with confidence when facing off against Pigtroopers, but, in reality, he often has no idea of what he is doing.

TERRIFYING TEREBACCA

Tall Terebacca may appear scary with his loud growls, but he is really as gentle as a mouse . . . or bird.

FALCON

Ham has made some of his own modifications to his spaceship to make it a better match for the Pig Empire's own ships.

BLASTER

Ham Solo doesn't like lightsabers. He prefers his trusty blaster. It fits perfectly in his belt holster, too.

REBEL PILOTS

The angry Rebel Birds can't wait to strap on their pilot helmets, jump into their spaceships, and attack the Pig Army. Red Skywalker leads the Rebel Bird pilots in their battered X-wing Birdfighter ships as they fly through the galaxy. Hang on tight—let's fly at 'em!

X-WING BIRDFIGHTER
Red pilots his Birdfighter while R2-EGG2 sits in back as his faithful droid co-pilot. What a simply cracking team!

ATTACK SHIP
The Rebel Bird pilots fly their Birdfighters in attack squadrons. Although sometimes they can't quite control their spaceships.

BIRD LEADER

Even though Red Skywalker is hardheaded and a little clumsy, he is one of the best Birdfighter pilots in the galaxy.

BLUE SQUADRON

The Blue Squadron team always back up their squadron leader. They are never discouraged though they are often exhausted!

CAN'T THEY GUESS FROM MY NAME THAT I'M THE EGG? GUESS THE YOLK'S ON THEM!

DROID PILOT

If only Red knew that his own co-pilot was the very thing that everyone was looking for: the mysterious and powerful Egg itself!

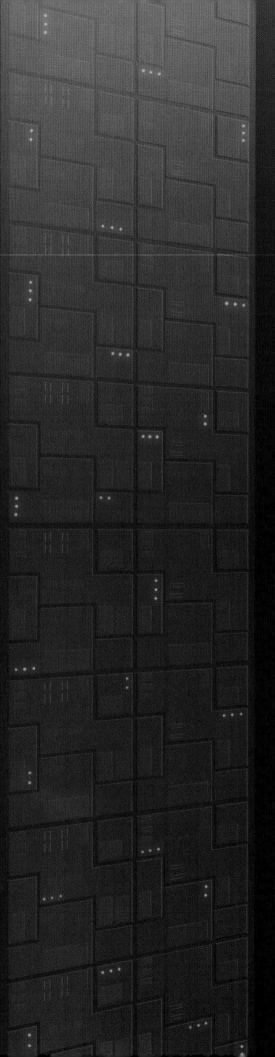

I WANT THIS WHOLE BOTTOMLESS SHAFT TO BE FILLED WITH CANDY AND JUNK FOOD . . . OR STICKERS!

Jedi Birds

Red Skywalker is learning to be a Jedi. Obi-Wan Kaboomi is already a Jedi. Yoda Bird is the greatest Jedi there is. It seems that everyone wants to be a Jedi. The Jedi are warriors with special, if unpredictable, powers! And even though they are powerful, Jedi often need a little help from their friends.

Jedi Red

Red is always so busy being a Jedi, he never seems to notice that Yoda Bird keeps trying to share the secret of The Egg.

Proud Jedi

Jedi Obi-Wan loves using the Force but can't always control his explosions.

You still have much to learn, young Red Jedi!

MASTER YODA BIRD

Old Jedi Master Yoda Bird hid The Egg inside R2-EGG2. He wants to share this secret but is getting absent-minded in his old age.

LIGHTSABER

The Jedi Birds fight using their traditional weapon, the lightsaber. A good Jedi Bird's lightsaber blade is blue.

FRIEND TO THE JEDI

C-3PYOLK is programmed to be on the side of the Jedi Birds— and to take care of plants whenever he sees one!

READY AND WILLING

With his lightsaber at his side, Obi-Wan Kaboomi is always ready to protect The Egg—even though he has no idea where it is!

HOTH

The conflict between the angry birds and the pigs has spread to many remote regions of the galaxy. However, none of them is as remote as the ice-cold plant of Hoth, which is not much more than a planet-sized snowball floating in deep space. It's lucky the birds have their feathers to keep warm.

WHY DID THE CHICKEN WALKER CROSS THE ROAD? TO BLAST SOME BIRDS!

SNOW WALKER
The pigs plan to walk all over the birds with these AT-AT walkers. A Pig Pilot drives it through the snow. Stomp, stomp!

CHICKEN WALKER
Special Pig Pilots drive these small, agile AT-ST walkers. They run around like crazy chickens, if chickens had blasters . . .

FRIENDS INDEED

Ham may not always laugh at Red's jokes, but one thing they do agree on is the need to protect the galaxy from greedy pigs.

PRINCESS POWER

Princess Stella wants to make sure the pigs don't take over the galaxy. And she doesn't mind squawking about it.

SNOW TROOPER

With special snow visors to keep pesky snowflakes out of their delicate snouts, Snow Troopers are designed for ice combat!

STICKERS

Ready for battle

Space station

Angry princess

Fatt backpack

Co-pilot Terebacca

Egg seekers

Vader in charge

Red Skywalker

Pilot pranks

Professional pilot

Stella star

Lightsaber

Yoda Bird

Launch pilot

Chuck

Vader

Hoth Obi-Wan

STICKERS

GROWLER

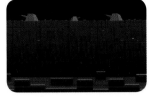

READY FOR SNOW

VIEW FROM THE BRIDGE

SCAREDY PIG

TIRED PILOT

SNOW ON SNOW

LARD VADER

LAUGHING RED

FIGHT IT OUT

BLASTER SOLO

MECHANIC TEREBACCA

PIG AND CHICKEN

PLEASED TROOPER

PIG STAR

WISE OBI

SKYWALKER ATTACK

OUTER SPACE OBI

CONFUSED RED

STICKERS

Pig Pilot

Into Battle

Red

Laughing Obi

Laughing Terebacca

Stella

Boba Fatt

Red's co-pilot

Rookie Rebel Bird

Bang!

Red and Blue

Red vs. Vader

Cold Terebacca

Pigtroopers

Princess Organa

STICKERS

Cloaked Kaboomi

Go, pigs!

Masked pilot

Sleepy Skywalker

Jedi Warrior

Chuck Solo

Pilot Skywalker

Red pig

Pig space station

Focused Red

Golden C-3PYOLK

Pig Commander

Egg droid

Feathery Rebel Bird

Pirate and Princess

Take that!

Smuggler Ham

STICKERS

Eyes Sharp

Ready Red

Pigs in space

Kaboomi

Tired Obi

Blasting Solo

Obi-Wan Kaboomi

Happy trooper

Chicken walker

R2-EGG2

Local bird

Hoth Walker

Snow walker

STICKERS

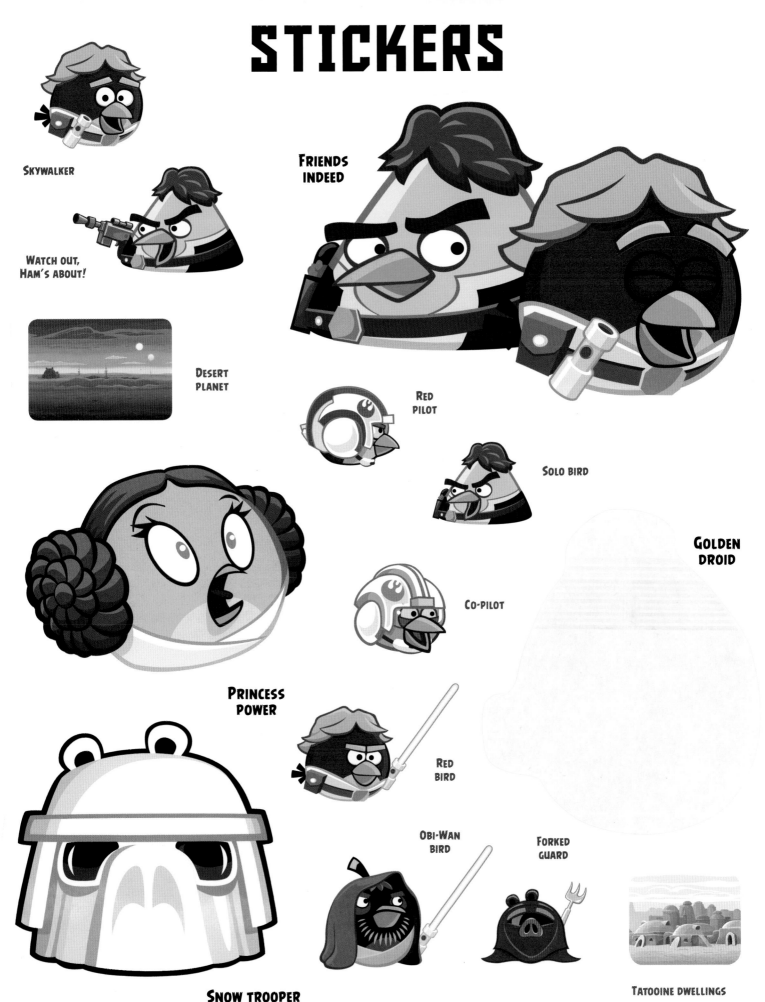

SKYWALKER

WATCH OUT, HAM'S ABOUT!

FRIENDS INDEED

DESERT PLANET

RED PILOT

SOLO BIRD

GOLDEN DROID

CO-PILOT

PRINCESS POWER

RED BIRD

OBI-WAN BIRD

FORKED GUARD

SNOW TROOPER

TATOOINE DWELLINGS

STICKERS

Viewer

Troopers

Ruffled feathers

Flying bird

Winged Jedi

Lightsaber ready!

Surprising Solo

Emperor Piglatine

Jedi Red

Speeding bird

Imperial Recruit

R2-EGG2's bird buddy

Proud Jedi

STICKERS

Master Yoda Bird

Feathered Jedi

Zooming Red

Sky-high

Greedo

In a flap

Eye on the prize

Sleeping Pilot

Red guards

Snow walking

Red lightsaber

Ready and willing

Friend to the Jedi

Solo Solo

STICKERS

Obi-Wan on Tatooine

Egg in his sights

Sign of the Empire

TIE in the sky

Commander pig

Traveling buddies

Pow!

Feathered Yoda

Happy Pig

Face of fear

Vader

Put your trotters up!

Shining C-3PYolk and Clever Egg

Pig rivals

STICKERS

SNOW PIG

TIE FIGHTER

WINGED PILOT RED

CLUMSY RED

STARING TEREBACCA

EVIL VADER

BATTLE READY

SECRET CHAMBER

POWERFUL OBI-WAN

PEACEFUL DROID

REPUBLIC LEADER

EXPLOSIVE KABOOMI

VADER'S VEHICLE

JUNK FOOD SMUGGLER

STICKERS

Confident Chuck

Under fire

Ham and blaster

Proud warrior

Pretty princess

Rebel Red Bird

In command

Lard leader

Pecking pilot

Forgetful Yoda

Close buddies

Tatooine's twin suns

Tired Terebacca

Desert Red

Ham's ship

And fire!

Falcon in flight

Dusty landscape

STICKERS

GROWLING BIRD

CONFIDENT BIRD

OUTER SPACE

HAM SMUGGLER

TERRIFYING TEREBACCA

SLURP!

CHIRPY KABOOMI

FALCON

CRACKING UP

WORRIED TROOPER

OUCH!

THE EMPEROR

EGG PROTECTOR

STICKERS

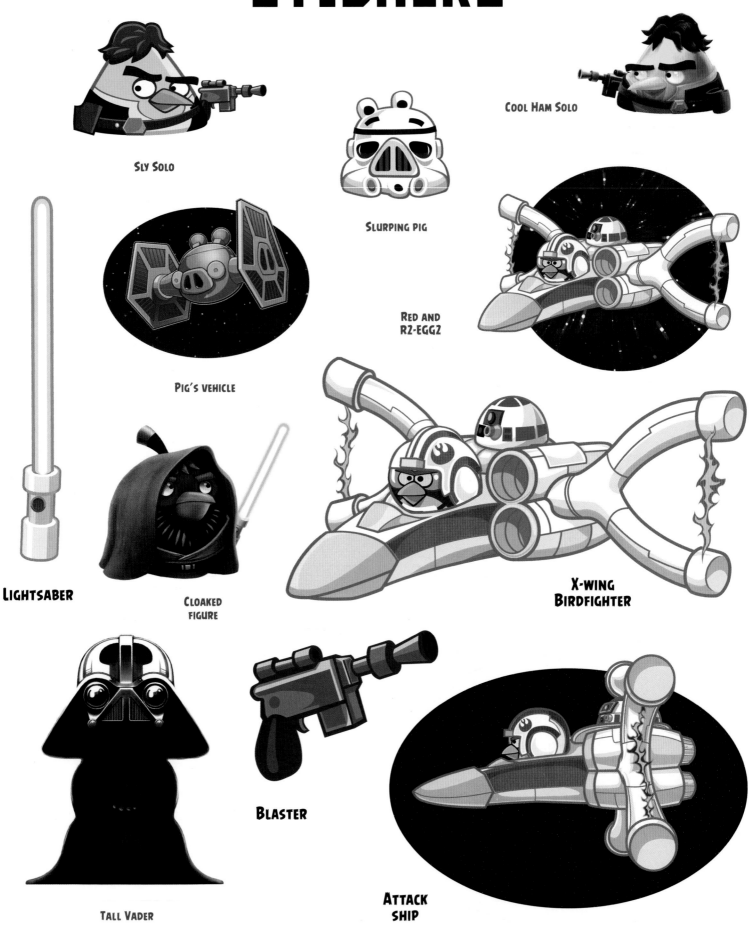

Sly Solo

Cool Ham Solo

Slurping pig

Red and
R2-EGG2

Pig's vehicle

Lightsaber

Cloaked
figure

X-wing
Birdfighter

Tall Vader

Blaster

Attack
ship

STICKERS

TATOOINE R2-EGG2

VADER IN CHARGE

BIRD LEADER

FRAZZLED HAM

ALARMED RED

VADER'S TIE

BLUE SQUADRON

SOLO'S BUDDY

DROID PILOT

UNRUFFLED RED

CHUCKLING CHUCK

ORGANA

PILOT IN SPACE

STICKERS

STICKERS

EXTRA STICKERS

EXTRA STICKERS

EXTRA STICKERS

EXTRA STICKERS

EXTRA STICKERS

EXTRA STICKERS

EXTRA STICKERS

EXTRA STICKERS

EXTRA STICKERS

EXTRA STICKERS

EXTRA STICKERS

EXTRA STICKERS

EXTRA STICKERS

EXTRA STICKERS

EXTRA STICKERS

EXTRA STICKERS